Ubuntu
Advanced Recovery Coach Professional Academy

I am because We are!

Marti Steiner
John Unger II

Copyright © 2023 by Marti Steiner and John Unger II

Editors: Xavier Hersom, Ricky Brown

Front Cover Photo: Amanda Johnson

All Rights Reserved. No part of this book may be used or reproduced by any means, graphic, electronic, or mechanical, including photocopying, recording, taping, or by any information storage retrieval system without the written permission of the publisher except in the case of brief quotations embodied in critical articles and reviews.

Third Edition

ISBN: 979-8-218-15265-9

Greater Recovery and Community Empowerment

Greater Recovery and Community Empowerment (GRaCE) is a 501c3 non-profit that was born in response to the devastating floods in southern West Virginia in 2016. Utilizing Asset Based Community Development, GRaCE offered a platform where people came together and worked as a community with individuals as they navigated recovery from that flood. In 2018 GRaCE shifted its focus and began training Life Coaches with a specialty in Recovery to address addiction in our communities. Since then, thousands have both found employment and have developed as leaders volunteering as Coaches and being advocates in their communities. We look forward to working with you as you are empowered to walk with your community as it heals and becomes stronger.

Advanced Recovery Coach Academy

Classes are 8am-4pm

Day 1
*Welcome
*Introductions
*Class Working Agreement
*Morals
(Break)
*Values
*Principles
(Break-Lunch)
*Ethics
*Documentary

Day 2
*Understanding Roles & Boundaries
*What is a Recovery/Life Coach
*Federal Definition of a Recovery Coach
(Break)
*Role Play
*Professionalism
*Accountability
(Break-Lunch)
*Appearance

Day 3
*Etiquette
*Stigma & Language
(Break)
*Demeanor & Poise
(Break-Lunch)
*Ethical Considerations
*Principles & Guidelines
*Legal Considerations
*Fiduciary Relationship
*Ethical Decisions

Day 4
*Ethical Scenarios
*Personal/Social Considerations
(Break)
*Boundaries
*Organization in Professionalism
(Break-Lunch)
*Motivational Interviewing
*Utilize SMART Goals
*SMART Goals
*Crisis Coaching
*SBIRT
*Role Plays

Day 5
*ED RC Job Description
*Ethical Assumptions
(Break)
*Ethical Consideration in the Judicial System
(Break-Lunch)
*Role Plays-Judicial System
*Recovery Support Professionals
*Next Steps-SMART Goal

Introductions, cont.

We are excited that you are interested in becoming a Recovery Coach Professional. This training is an intense, fast paced five-day class. At the completion of this class, you will become one of the 'special forces' in the Recovery Coach community-you will not only understand and demonstrate the importance of ethics and professionalism as a Recovery Coach, but also what it takes to work or volunteer in crisis and professional settings.

Being a coach is to walk with someone as they become better. That might mean the person you are working with is considering making huge changes in their life as they navigate their recovery. Our goal as a coach is to ultimately empower the coachee to choose a path to change, and how to find the resources they need to do so. This is done through asking good questions and believing in the coachees capacity for change-giving hope.

Being a Recovery Coach Professional is a serving role. As people become better, communities become stronger. By taking this class, you will have the opportunity to become part of a large network of Recovery Coach Professionals dedicated to helping folks in their own community and supporting each other.

We look forward to working with you!

Marti Steiner Unger
John Unger

Objectives for Recovery Coach Professional

Upon completion of this course, students will be able to:

- Describe the role of the Recovery Coach Professional (RCP) and its functions
- List the components of and the importance of SMART goals
- Explain accountability in the Recovery Coach Professional role
- Build skills to coach in crisis situations.
- Describe the importance of appearance as a Recovery Coach
- Explain the importance of reliability
- Apply active listening and motivational interviewing
- Explore ethics and boundaries
- Discover attitudes about stigma in different settings
- Explain ethical decision making
- Describe principles, morals, and values
- Increase awareness of the importance of etiquette and demeanor
- Explore case studies and ethical considerations in different settings
- Describe SBIRT and its application to coaching
- Examine ethical guidelines for the delivery of peer-based recovery support services
- Describe accountability and its importance
- Explain the importance of maintaining poise as an RCP
- Describe advocacy and its importance
- Practice newly acquired skills

- Students who successfully complete the Recovery/Life Coach I and the Recovery Coach Professional training will receive:

- A Skill Set Certificate of Completion from the college in which this course is taken as a Recovery Coach Professional (RCP).

- The designation of Recovery Coach Professional by Greater Recovery and Community Empowerment (GRaCE).

As more entities (hospitals, providers, courts, prisons, etc...) employ Recovery Coaches, an RCP represents a level of competence and expertise, elevating the standards for Recovery Coaches in professional settings.

An RCP is proficient in the art and science of recovery coaching through actively listening, motivational interviewing, ethical considerations and guidelines, maintaining poise and demeanor in crisis environments, and of the importance of accountability and responsibility. These skills are essential as a Recovery Coach Professional.

Advanced Recovery Coach Professional Academy (ARCPA) includes:

- 20 hours of Ethics

- 10 hours of Professionalism

- 5 hours of Crisis (Emergency Dept.) Recovery Coaching

- 5 hours of Judicial Recovery Coaching

+ 55 Clinical/Field work hours required

The course includes 4 third party college credits

I Am because We Are
Ubuntu

Advanced Recovery Coach Professional Academy

Day 1

Copyright © 2020
Marti Steiner, RCP
John Unger, RCP
All Rights Reserved.

Class Introductions

Please introduce yourself with the following:

- Your name
- Where you are from
- Why you are taking this class

Class Working Agreement

A class working agreement helps define expectations in class.

What kind of learning environment do we want to have? How do we attain that?

What guidelines do we want to include?

Let's spend a few moments and develop a class working agreement.

Morals

Write your definition of morals.

_____
_____
_____
_____
_____
_____
_____
_____

Write your group definition of morals.

_____
_____
_____
_____
_____
_____
_____
_____

Morals, cont.

: of or relating to principles of right and wrong in behavior
: conforming to a standard of right behavior
: sanctioned by or operative on one's conscience or ethical judgment
: capable of right and wrong action

Merriam-Webster. (n.d.). Moral. In *Merriam-Webster.com dictionary*. Retrieved July 21, 2020, from https://www.merriamwebster.com/dictionary/moral

Let's watch a short video explaining morals.
https://www.youtube.com/watch?v=0WxOGR6HKFs

Values

Write your definition of values.

_____
_____
_____
_____
_____
_____
_____

Write your group definition of values.

_____
_____
_____
_____
_____
_____
_____

Values, cont.

: something (such as a principle or quality) intrinsically valuable or desirable

Merriam-Webster. (n.d.). Value. In *Merriam-Webster.com dictionary*. Retrieved July 21, 2020, from https://www.merriamwebster.com/dictionary/value

These can be held by individuals, groups and communities.
What are some values held by individuals?

_____
_____
_____
_____
_____

What are values held by groups?

_____
_____
_____
_____
_____

What are values held by communities?

_____
_____
_____
_____
_____

Principle

Write your definition of principle.
_____
_____
_____
_____
_____
_____

Write your group definition of principle.
_____
_____
_____
_____
_____
_____
_____

Principle, cont.

: a comprehensive and fundamental law, doctrine, or assumption
: a rule or code of conduct

Merriam-Webster. (n.d.). Principle. In *Merriam-Webster.com dictionary*. Retrieved July 21, 2020, from https://www.merriamwebster.com/dictionary/principle

Why is it important that we understand morals, values and principles as a Recovery Coach Professional?

_____
_____
_____
_____
_____
_____
_____
_____
_____
_____
_____
_____
_____
_____
_____
_____
_____

Ethics

Think about what the term ethics means to you. Please write your personal definition of ethics below.

_____
_____
_____
_____
_____
_____
_____
_____

What is my group definition of ethics?

_____
_____
_____
_____
_____
_____
_____
_____

Ethics are-

: the discipline dealing with what is good and bad and with moral duty and obligation
: a set of moral principles: a theory or system of moral values
: the principles of conduct governing an individual or a group
: a guiding philosophy

"Ethic." *Merriam-Webster.com Dictionary*, Merriam-Webster, https://www.merriam-webster.com/dictionary/ethic Accessed 20 Jul. 2020.

Let's learn more about ethics.

Ethics, cont.

Iatrogenic harm is when the caregiver or provider unintentionally harms the person cared for during an intervention.

Can you think of examples of iatrogenic harm?
_____
_____
_____
_____

What might be an example of iatrogenic harm while coaching? Explain why?
_____
_____
_____
_____

Who else might be harmed by what a coach does, or does not do? What might be an example of multi-party vulnerability?
_____
_____
_____
_____

Ethics, cont.

Why are we discussing Ethics in Coaching?

Let's review.

It is important to think about possible outcomes of choices we make as Recovery Coach Professionals: ask for guidance from other Recovery Coach Professionals or your supervisor if you have ethical questions to avoid iatrogenic harm. Many times, we need to think a step beyond the initial response to the action (or non-action).

Now let us watch a documentary and think about ethical issues from many different viewpoints.

I Am because We Are
Ubuntu

Advanced Recovery Coach Professional Academy

Day 2

Copyright © 2020
Marti Steiner, RCP
John Unger, RCP
All Rights Reserved.

Understanding Roles and Boundaries

Let's review some different roles in the recovery community. It is important that we understand our role and stay in our lane when volunteering or working as a coach.

Education	Must complete college degree. Must complete license requirements and certification as required by state boards. Must recertify via continuing earning education credits.	Must complete training from and be vetted by a recovery community organization.	Must be in personal recovery. Minimal training, achieved through organizational approval.	Must be in personal recovery. Must complete government license requirements and certification as required by state boards. Must recertify via continuing earning education credits.
Service Dimension	Typically serves within a philosophy.	Empowers coachee to choose between multiple paths.	Serves within the organization's beliefs.	Work from perspective of their lived experience to help build environments conducive to recovery. [1]
Perception of Power	High difference in perception of power. Counselor is viewed as knowing what is best.	Possible moderate or minor, depending on the style of coaching, organization.	Minor or nonexistence.	Moderate to high, depending on organization. Viewed as having answers.
Formality of Helping	Formal, following specific ethical guidelines.	Formal, but personable, following specific ethical guidelines based on organizational setting.	Informal.	Formal, but personable, following specific ethical guidelines based on organizational setting.
Use of self in relationship.	Prohibited in most cases.	Discouraged. Complete service role expected.	Accepted, lived experience standard expectation.	Accepted, lived experience standard expectation
Focus on the past, present, future.	Primarily focuses on past.	Focuses on the present and future.	Variable.	Focuses on the present and future.
Advocacy	Minimal	Significant	Minimal	Significant
Compensation	Paid position.	Paid or volunteer position.	Volunteer position.	Paid Position.

1. "Certified Peer Specialist Job Description" Georgia Peer Specialist Certification Project. March 2003. www.gmhcn.org/cps-job-description

Recovery/Life Coach

What is a Recovery/Life Coach?

A Recovery/Life Coach is someone who empowers the coachee as they transform from who they are today, to the person they want to become.

Who can be a coach?

Anyone interested and trained in walking with someone as they improve themselves. This is accomplished in an unbiased, ethical, and professional manner.

What does a Recovery/Life Coach do?

- **Listen** (and ask good questions).
- **Empower** (the coachee to find resources).
- **Believe** (the coachee can change, share hope).
- **Advocate** (with the coachee and community).

What a coach does *not* do.

- Judge (coaches must always be aware of their own biases).
- Give advice (the pathway to change is always up to the coachee).
- Become friends (coaches are friendly but must maintain good boundaries).

Federal Definition of a Recovery Coach

H.R. 6, SUPPORT for Patients and Communities Act, which was enacted by Congress and signed by the President on Oct 24, 2018. The analogous provisions in the Support Act appear to be these: Subtitle I—Preventing Overdoses While in Emergency Rooms; Sec. 7081. Program to support coordination and continuation of care for drug overdose patients.

This subsection requires the Secretary of DHHS to "award grants on a competitive basis to eligible entities to support implementation of voluntary programs for care and treatment of individuals after a drug overdose, as appropriate, which may include implementation of the best practices described in subsection (a), which includes "(1)emergency treatment of known or suspected drug overdose; (2)the use of recovery coaches, as appropriate, to encourage individuals who experience a non-fatal overdose to seek treatment for substance use disorder and to support coordination and continuation of care; (3)coordination and continuation of care and treatment, including, as appropriate, through referrals, of individuals after a drug overdose; and (4)the provision or prescribing of overdose reversal medication, as appropriate."

For purposes of this subsection a "recovery coach" is defined in section (c)(2) as "an individual—

(A)with knowledge of, or experience with, recovery from a substance use disorder; and
(B)who has completed training from, and is determined to be in good standing by, a recovery services organization capable of conducting such training and making such determination."

In breakout rooms: considering the role and definition of a Recovery Coach, what may be ethically challenging issues that could come up while coaching? List and share why.

Please designate a recorder/reporter to share what your group discussed.

Professionalism

What are characteristics of a professional?

_____
_____
_____
_____
_____

In your small group, come up with a definition for a professional and for professionalism. Please designate someone to record and report your group's definition.

_____
_____
_____
_____
_____
_____
_____
_____

Professionalism, cont.

Definition of *professional*

: of, relating to, or characteristic of a profession
: engaged in one of the learned professions
: characterized by or conforming to the technical or ethical standards of a profession
: exhibiting a courteous, conscientious, and generally businesslike manner in the workplace

Definition of *professionalism*

: **the conduct, aims, or qualities** that characterize or mark a profession or a professional person.

Merriam-Webster. (n.d.). Professional and Professionalism. In *Merriam-Webster.com dictionary*. Retrieved July 25, 2020, from https://www.merriam-webster.com/dictionary/professionalism

Reflection: Is it important for a Recovery Coach to be viewed as professional? Explain your answer.

Accountability

As a Recovery Coach Professional, we are accountable to many different groups. In the context of a coach that works in the medical field, please answer the following questions.

Please list to whom we are accountable too. Rank your list in order of importance.

_____
_____
_____
_____
_____
_____
_____

Would these groups view us in a positive, or negative light? Explain.

_____
_____
_____
_____
_____
_____
_____

Accountability, cont.

In the context of a coach that works in the judicial system, please list to whom we are accountable to. Please rank your list in order of importance.

_____
_____
_____
_____
_____
_____
_____
_____
_____

Reflection: Why is it important that we understand accountability?

_____
_____
_____
_____
_____
_____
_____
_____

Appearance

Recovery Coaches need to be aware that appearances are important! Please reflect on the following three questions as you look at each individual to follow.

Is this Recovery Coach's appearance:

Appropriate for a Community Recovery Coach?
Why?

Appropriate for a Recovery Coach Professional in the medical setting?
Why?

Appropriate for a Recovery Coach Professional working in the judicial system?
Why?

Recovery Coach #	Community Recovery Coach	Recovery Coach Working in the Medical Field	Recovery Coach Working in the Judicial System
1			
2			
3			
4			
5			
6			

1

2

3

4

5

6

First Impressions

First impressions matter, for good and bad. They are fine when you like someone on first meeting; they are not so fine when the first meeting is negative. Positive first impressions lead to social cohesion; negative first impressions lead to biases and social prejudice.

Arthur Dobrin DSW. (n.d.). The Power of the First Impression. Retrieved July 23, 2020, from
https://www.psychologytoday.com/us/blog/am-i-right/201302/the-power-first-impressions

You have a specific identity, whether by design or default. Your "professional presence"—or your lack of it—is the sum of the qualities that others perceive in you. It has a powerful impact on whether your individual contributions positively or negatively impact the goals, mission, and vision of your organization.

When others interact with you, you need to be certain they get a true picture of your core values, skill sets and competencies.

Anon. (n.d.) Employees-First Impressions. Retrieved July 20th from 2020
http://employeedevelopmentsystems.com/resources/ideacasts/firstimpressions-and-professionalism/

Considering the context of where we work or volunteer, and who we are accountable to, it is important that Recovery Coaches make a good first impression.

First Impressions, cont.

Consider the following:

-The environment (is it safe or appropriate to wear long earrings, open toed-shoes, long necklaces?)

-Personal Grooming

-Is there policy concerning tattoos, piercings, or hair color?

-Refraining from wearing clothes that reveal undergarments (exposed bra straps, low pants, etc).

What else might we consider?
_____
_____
_____
_____
_____
_____
_____
_____
_____

First Impressions, cont.

What might be some sample dress codes for the following?

Community Recovery Coach

_____
_____
_____
_____
_____
_____

Recovery Coach Professionals in the Emergency Department dress code

_____
_____
_____
_____
_____
_____

Recovery Coach Professional working/volunteering in the Judicial System

_____
_____
_____
_____
_____
_____

I Am because We Are
Ubuntu

Advanced Recovery Coach Professional Academy

Day 3

Etiquette

Professional etiquette is an unwritten code of conduct regarding the interactions among the members in a business setting. When proper professional etiquette is used, all involved are able to feel more comfortable, and things tend to flow more smoothly. In professional situations, displaying proper etiquette can give you a competitive edge over others who may not be using proper etiquette. Likewise, failing to use the correct etiquette may result in being overlooked for employment or losing other valuable opportunities. Professional etiquette can be applied to many areas of an individual's work life including e-mails, phone calls, and business meetings.

Anon. (n.d.) Professional etiquette in the workplaces. Retrieved July 21st from 2020
https://career.uccs.edu/resources/students/professionaletiquette-in-the-workplace

Let's look at a few scenarios.

1. Your cell phone rings during a session with a coachee. Do you answer your phone? Explain

2. A Recovery Coach shares gossip about another Recovery Coach. What do you do?

3. Your coachee begins to cry while sharing past trauma. You feel the urge to give them a hug. What do you do?

4. Your coachee introduces you to their significant other. What do you do?

5. Your coachee does not arrive on time for their appointment. What do you do?

6. You need to send an email to a coachee. How do you start your email?

7. You have a bad day while volunteering or working as a Recovery Coach and are considering venting on social media. What do you do?

8. You have a project due tomorrow at work but have been invited to a holiday event. You need to finish the project, but you know you would enjoy the event. What do you do?

Etiquette, cont.

In your breakout room, come up with a scenario that might depict poor etiquette by a Recovery Coach. Please designate a recorder/reporter to share what your group came up with.

_____
_____
_____
_____
_____
_____
_____

Reflection: What does good professional etiquette look like for a Recovery Coach Professional? Create a list.

_____
_____
_____
_____
_____
_____
_____
_____

Stigma and Language

As we discussed in RCLCI, using appropriate language as a Recovery Coach Professional is especially important. Using appropriate language reduces stigma to people we are speaking to or about.

What common language fosters stigma and what do we want to replace it with? *Ex. Clean/Dirty with Positive/Negative

_____
_____
_____
_____
_____
_____
_____

What is language that supports and empowers people in recovery? *Ex. Instead of calling yourself an "addict", replace with "I suffer an addiction" or "I am in recovery" (Person first language, not the disease)

_____
_____
_____
_____
_____
_____
_____

Stigma and Language, cont.

Discussion:

What are forms of stigma for people seeking professional services?

What are ways Recovery Coach Professionals can reduce stigma?

How can Recovery Coach Professionals be advocates in professional settings?

Demeanor and Poise

Let's look at the definition of demeanor and poise.

Demeanor
: behavior toward others : outward manner

Poise
: easy self-possessed assurance of manner
: gracious tact in coping or handling
: a particular way of carrying oneself

"Poise and Demeanor." *Merriam-Webster.com Dictionary*, Merriam-Webster, https://www.merriam-webster.com/dictionary/poise Accessed 27 Jul. 2020.

Brainstorm ways to demonstrate professional demeanor and poise.

_____
_____
_____
_____

What are ways **NOT** to illustrate demeanor.

_____
_____
_____
_____

Demeanor and Poise, cont.

Let's look at a couple of scenarios...

Maxine is a staff member of the court in which you volunteer for as a Recovery Coach Professional. She is constantly complaining to other staff about how "the town is full of addicts and how they have ruined the community," and has told you on multiple occasions "good luck, they will never change."

How do you respond to this scenario as a Recovery Coach Professional?

_____
_____
_____
_____

You have been notified of a coachee requesting an RCP in the Emergency Department. When you arrive, the ED is terribly busy. You sign in and are told what room to go to. The coachee is with family members who demand that you 'fix' the coachee and do not want to leave the room, and the nurse steps into the room for a moment, rolls her eyes, and immediately leaves the room.

How do you respond to this scenario as a Recovery Coach Professional?

_____
_____
_____
_____

Ethical Considerations

Ethical decisions generate and sustain trust; demonstrate respect, responsibility, fairness and caring; and are consistent with good citizenship. These behaviors provide a foundation for making better decisions by setting the ground rules for our behavior.

UC San Diego (April 4, 2014). Making Ethical Decisions: Process. Retrieved on July 27th, 2020.
https://blink.ucsd.edu/finance/accountability/ethics/process.html

Three simple principles can help you make better decisions.

1. **All decisions must take into account and reflect a concern for the interests and well-being of all affected individuals ("stakeholders").**
The underlying principle here is the Golden Rule —help when you can, avoid harm when you can.

2. **Ethical values and principles *always* take precedence over non-ethical ones.**
Ethical values are morally superior to non-ethical ones. When faced with a clear choice between such values, the ethical person should always choose to follow ethical principles.

3. **It is ethically proper to violate an ethical principle only when it is clearly necessary to advance another true ethical principle, which, according to the decision-maker's conscience, will produce the greatest balance of good in the long run.**

Some decisions will require you to prioritize and to choose between competing ethical values and principles when it is clearly necessary to do so because the only viable options require the sacrifice of one ethical value over another ethical value. When this is the case, the decisionmaker should act in a way that will create the greatest amount of good and the least amount of harm to the greatest number of people.

©2000 Josephson Institute of Ethics http://josephsoninstitute.org/UC San Diego (April 4, 2014). Making Ethical Decisions: Process. Retrieved on July 27th, 2020.
https://blink.ucsd.edu/finance/accountability/ethics/model.html

Six Core Ethical Values and Supporting Ethical Principles

Core Ethical Values	Supporting Ethical Principles
Trustworthiness	truthfulness, sincerity, candor integrity, promise keeping, loyalty, honesty
Respect	respect, autonomy, courtesy, self-determination
Responsibility	responsibility, diligence, continuous improvement, self-restraint
Fairness	justice, fairness, impartiality, equality
Caring	caring, kindness, compassion
Citizenship	citizenship, philanthropy, voting

Principles and Guidelines

A Recovery Coach Professional's sole mission is to empower individuals and families in recovering from addiction and its related issues by overcoming obstacles to recovery and work with each individual and family to discover resources within and beyond themselves to both initiate and sustain the recovery process. RCP's actions will be guided by the following core recovery values and service guidelines:

Gratitude and Service —Serving with an attitude of gratitude (and humility) is at the core of RCP's purpose.

Personal Recovery —RCP's are aware of and share the importance of self-care. You must take care of yourself first before you can help others.

Face and Voice of Recovery —RCP's are good role models and leaders in the recovery community.

Self-Improvement —RCP's foster continuous self-improvement.

Honesty —RCP's tell the truth and when wrong will admit it and work towards reconciliation.

Authenticity —RCP's carry the recovery message in both word and deed.

Keeping Promises —RCP's keep their word.

Humility —RCP's work within limitations, handle disagreements respectfully, and seek help when needed.

Principles and Guidelines, cont.

Loyalty —RCP's serve and behave in ways that uplift the recovery and general community.

Hope —RCP's help others focus on their assets, strengths, and recovery possibilities.

Respect —RCP's honor the imperfections of others and themselves while always treating those seeking recovery as resources with dignity.

Acceptance —RCP's acknowledge there are many pathways to recovery however diverse, even those they may personally oppose.

Recovery Integrity —RCP's carrying the message of empowering the recovery of others but are humble enough to realize they cannot carry the person.

Protection —RCP's do no harm by respecting privacy and refraining from gossip. They avoid all forms of exploitation or harassment of those they serve. Their relationships are sanctuaries of safety.

Advocacy —RCP's reduce stigma by promoting connection to resources with the coachee and others.

Stewardship —RCPs use or create resources in the wisest way possible to provide benefits others need to achieve recovery.

Based on White, W., the PRO-ACT Ethics Workgroup, with legal discussion by PopovitsR. & Donohue, B. (2007). Ethical Guidelines for the Delivery of Peer-based Recovery Support Services. Philadelphia: Philadelphia Department of Behavioral Health and Mental Retardation Services.

Ethical Dilemma

Now, let's look at a common **ethical dilemma**.

-You find a $10 bill at Wal-Mart. What do you do?

To make an **ethical decision** think about:

-Who are the affected parties?

-What rights to those parties have?

-What action is fair and does not show discrimination?

-What action advances the common good?

-What action develops ethical moral values?

Your facilitator will lead a discussion on ethical decision making.

Legal Considerations

HIPAA

The Health Insurance Portability and Accountability Act of 1996 (HIPAA) is a federal law that required the creation of national standards to protect sensitive patient health information from being disclosed without the patient's consent or knowledge. The US Department of Health and Human Services (HHS) issued the HIPAA Privacy Rule to implement the requirements of HIPAA. The HIPAA Security Rule protects a subset of information covered by the Privacy Rule.

Mandated Reporting

There are crises that demand immediate action on our part. As a Recovery/Life Coach you are a mandated reporter.

This means you will need to immediately report the following:

If you suspect or have reason to believe that a child or elderly person has been abused or neglected, the coachee intends to hurt someone or if the coachee is suicidal.

This law is in place to protect vulnerable populations.
If the person you are coaching discloses anything that is mandated to be reported, make sure you are in a safe place before doing so.
If the coachee is suicidal, encourage them to call a suicide hotline while you stay with them (and stay with them until they receive professional help). If the coachee refuses and eventually leaves the meeting, **call 911.**

Document what, when, where and who was involved and inform your place of business, or the institution/organization where you are working/volunteering at as a coach. Resources for reporting in West Virginia-

*Abuse and Neglect Hotline (1-800-352-6513) 7 days a week, 24 hours a day.
*911
*1-844-HELP-4-WV (844-435-7498)

In breakout rooms, develop a short 5-minute (realistic) roleplay illustrating mandated reporting in a coaching session.

Fiduciary relationship

: of, relating to, or involving a confidence or trust:
: held or founded in trust or confidence

Merriam-Webster. (n.d.). Fiduciary. In *Merriam-Webster.com dictionary*. Retrieved July 28, 2020, from https://www.merriamwebster.com/dictionary/fiduciary

A fiduciary relationship encompasses the idea of faith and confidence and is generally only when the confidence given by one person is actually accepted by the other person. All of the fiduciary's actions are performed for the advantage of the beneficiary.

fiduciary. (n.d.) *West's Encyclopedia of American Law, edition 2.* (2008). Retrieved July 28 2020 from https://legaldictionary.thefreedictionary.com/Fiduciary

Reflection-is the power differential between a Recovery Coach and a coachee really equal? Why?

_____
_____
_____
_____
_____

Reflection-why is it important that we understand fiduciary relationships, iatrogenic harm, multi-parti vulnerability and boundaries?

_____
_____
_____
_____
_____

Ethical Decisions

Review-

To make an ethical decision think about:
-Who are the affected parties?
-What rights to those parties have?
-What action is fair and is not biased?
-What action advances the common good?
-What action develops ethical moral values?

Thinking about what we have learned, please complete the following checklist.

	Should a Recovery Coach… their coachee?	Yes	Maybe	Never
1	Give a hug to			
2	Accept a gift from			
3	Give a gift to			
4	Accept an invitation to a special occasion from			
5	Have a relationship with			
6	Hire			
7	Say "you're very attractive" to			
8	Share their phone number with			
9	Accept a personal social media friend request from			
10	Lend money to			

I Am because We Are
Ubuntu

Advanced Recovery Coach Professional Academy

Day 4

Copyright © 2020
Marti Steiner, RCP
John Unger, RCP
All Rights Reserved

Ethical Scenarios

Cathie, (your coachee) is a single mother who works full time, attends college part time and is financially challenged. She has been solid in her recovery from an addiction for 1.5 years. She meets you for your coaching session at a restaurant at 5:30pm with her two young children and her children persistently complain about being hungry. Cathie explains that her babysitter was unexpectantly sick and her mother watched her children while she was at work. Unfortunately, her mother did not have food to feed her children. Cathie confides that she did not feed her children before dropping them off at her mother's, as her babysitter would feed her children all three meals while she worked and went to school. Cathie begins to cry as she shares that she cannot afford to purchase food until she is paid from her job in two days.

What do you do? What is the reasoning behind your answers?

_____
_____
_____
_____
_____
_____
_____
_____
_____
_____
_____

Personal/Social Considerations in Coaching

Joe is a recovery coach in a small town. He is a well-respected volunteer coach and is known for providing great coaching support for his coachees. Six months ago, Joe became a pastor at a local church and garnished media attention because of a certain religious view he holds. While volunteering as a coach, Joe does not promote any specific religious view, however this heightened awareness of his religious position has drawn the attention of partners of the organization, co-workers, and the non-profit that Joe volunteers for.

What ethical considerations does this scenario highlight?

_____
_____
_____
_____
_____
_____
_____
_____
_____

Boundaries

Knowing the differences between personal and professional relationships can help you recognize when professional boundaries between the two may be blurred or crossed.

Characteristic	Professional	Personal
Behavior	Regulated by a code of ethics and professional standards. Framed by organizational policy. More private, less emotional (less conversation about politics, religion, personal life, etc)	Guided by personal values and beliefs. More intimate and emotional. Friendships.
Remuneration	May be paid but may also act in a volunteer role.	No payment for being in the relationship.
Length	Time-limited.	May last a lifetime.
Location	Place defined and limited to where coaching is provided.	Place unlimited; often undefined.
Purpose	Provides coaching within a defined role. Less accessible.	Pleasure, interest directed. More accessible.
Structure	Provides care/service to client.	Spontaneous, unstructured.
Power	Unequal: has more power due to perceived authority, knowledge, and influence.	Relatively equal.
Preparation for	Requires formal education, knowledge, preparation, orientation, and training.	Does not require formal knowledge, preparation, orientation, and training.
Time spent	Gives care within outlined hours of work/volunteerism.	Personal choice for how much time is spent in the relationship.

Adapted from Milgrom, J. (1992). *Boundaries in professional relationships: a training manual.* Minneapolis, Minnesota: Walk-In Counseling Centre.

Motivational Interviewing

In the previous class, we learned the basics of motivational interviewing. Let's review and practice.

Remember the four principles of MI:

    Expressing empathy.
    Developing discrepancy.
    Rolling with resistance.
    Supporting self-efficacy.

"Do you mind if we spend a few minutes talking about…?"
"What makes you think it might be time for a change?"
"What brought you here today?"
"What happens when you [issue]?"
"What was that like for you?"
"What's different about (accomplishing improvement) this time?"
"It sounds like…"
"It seems as if…"
"Explain to me how (taking an action) is supporting your goal of (…………)"
"What are the pro and cons of taking this action?"
"What I hear you saying…"
"I get the sense that…"

Are there any other good starts you might want to add?

Let's prepare for our next coaching section by reviewing SMART goals!

Utilize SMART Goals

S-Specific. Let the coachee come up with *exactly* what'.

Example: (Goal = Acquiring a Job)

NOT Specific-"I will apply for a job this week."
Specific-"I will apply **at Target, this Tuesday at 10am**."

M-Measurable. How much? There should be number involved.

Example: (Goal= Maintaining a Healthy Weight)

NOT Measurable-"I want to work out this week."
Measurable-"I want to exercise for **25 minutes**, **Monday, Wednesday, and Saturday** at 8am at Gold's Gym in Fairmont."

A-Achievable-Each goal needs to be attainable within time constraints.

-Many times, this means breaking larger goals into smaller ones.

Example: (Goal= Getting a Job as a Veterinarian)

NOT Achievable: "I want to become a veterinarian this summer."
Achievable: "On **Monday at 6pm I will apply online to Blue Ridge Community and Technical College** for their Veterinary Assistant Program."

R-Relevant-Why is this goal being set?
-Does it contribute to the 'ultimate goal'?

Example: (Goal= Being Financially Secure)

NOT Relevant-"I will talk to my mom at 9am for two hours on Friday."
Relevant-"I will **read "The Total Money Makeover" 30 minutes Monday, Wednesday, Thursday and Sunday** this week."

T-Time-Bound-Through good questioning, let the coachee choose the proper time parameter.

Example: (Goal= Acquiring a Driver's License)

NOT Time-Bound-"I will get my Driver's License this week."
Time Bound-"I will call the DMV to see what documentation I need to obtain my Driver's License, as well as any other paperwork or fees on **Thursday at 9am.**"

Writing good SMART goals takes practice for most people. Give examples and practice with the coachee.

Practice by writing a SMART Goal on the next page.

SMART Goals

Specific-What exactly is your goal?

_____

_____

Measurable-How much?

_____

_____

Achievable-Can you complete it?

_____

_____

Relevant-Do they align with your ultimate goal?

_____

_____

Time-Bound-Is it within a time frame you can work?

_____

_____

SMART Goal-Combine the points above into one SMART Goal!

_____

_____

_____

_____

Organization in Professionalism

Organization in Professionalism

1. What I can always find_____
2. What I have a specific space for_____
3. The space I feel is always organized_____
4. I am always on time for_____
5. I always have time for_____
6. I frequently misplace my_____
7. I don't have space for_____
8. The place that is always cluttered is_____
9. I am frequently late for_____
10. I never have time for_____

Why do you think being organized is beneficial as a Coach (or in life)?
https://youtu.be/88MjoZalHpM

Write a SMART Goal that you can utilize to become more organized in one area of your life.

Let's review Motivational Interviewing then get ready to coach!

Crisis Coaching

Crisis Coaching
Ex. Emergency Dept., QRT, Clinics, Detox

Crisis coaching is different than community coaching. As a crisis coach you will be with a coachee at a point in their life where they will need to answer the question "What's the next step, right now?" and walk with the coachee as they begin that path within that meeting.

What does a crisis coach do?

- A crisis coach will assist the coachee discern what path might work for them, they will **still not** give advice.
- However, the crisis coach may 'give' wanted resources at that moment.
- The crisis coach will continue to make follow up contact for a limited amount of time.
- The crisis coach will connect the coachee to a community coach.
- A crisis coach will maintain poise at all times.
- A crisis coach will remember who they are accountable to at all times and act in a professional capacity.

SBIRT

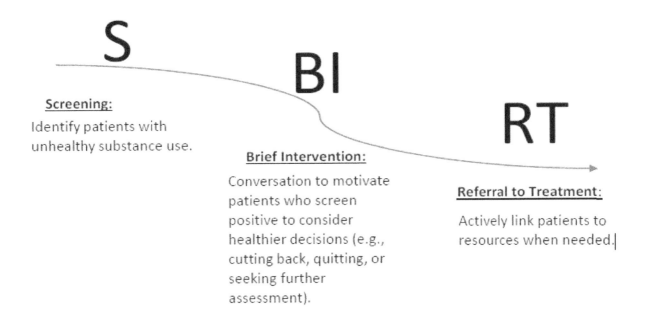

SBIRT has been defined by SAMHSA as a comprehensive, integrated, public health approach to the delivery of early intervention for individuals with risky alcohol and drug use, and the timely referral to more intensive substance use treatment for those who have substance abuse disorders. There is consensus that a comprehensive SBIRT model includes screening, brief intervention/brief treatment and referral to treatment. (SBIRT is typically used in crisis situations)

Why is it important for coaches to understand SBIRT?

Role Play

In breakout rooms, you will be designing a role play that takes place in an ED. You will need to have an RCP, a coachee and other speaking supporting parts. Your group will project either an RCP demonstrating professionalism by being poised, ethical, and organized *or* an RCP demonstrating poor professionalism (not being poised, ethical, organized, etc). You will have 20 minutes to come up with a role play to share.

I Am because We Are
Ubuntu

Advanced Recovery Coach Professional Academy

Day 5

Emergency Department Recovery Coach Job Description

Position Summary:

Qualifications:

Duties and Responsibilities:

Emergency Department Recovery Coach Description Position

Summary:

The ED Recovery Coach will provide recovery coaching services in hospital emergency departments serving as a motivator, resource broker and liaison.

Qualifications

- Recovery Coach/Life Coach I Certificate
- Recovery Coach Professional Certificate
- Spirituality in Coaching and Coaching through Grief certificates (preferred)
- Naloxone Certificate
- Experience with or knowledge of the recovery process
- Understand medication-assisted recovery and its practices
- Familiarity with local support services, resources and recovery community
- Capability of building an effective coach-coachee relationship
- Demonstrated skill in active listening, motivational interviewing and awareness of self and treating people as resources
- Understanding of and ability to maintain appropriate boundaries
- Ability to work in a hospital setting
- Availability to work different shifts as necessary
- Cross-cultural skills and experience with culturally diverse populations
- A valid driver's license, insurance and reliable vehicle required
- Must pass a background check
- Bilingual abilities are a plus
- Strong customer service ethic essential

Emergency Department Recovery Coach Description Position, cont.

Duties and Responsibilities

Follow up recovery coaching with ED recoverees for 10 days following initial contact

- Work closely with Emergency Department personnel and staff
- Facilitate timely referrals and placements from hospital to treatment/recovery support providers
- Connect patients to a larger community of care
- Engage in recovery planning with recoveree
- Educate and assist family members as requested
- Serve as a community ambassador
- Report writing, record keeping as required by GRaCE Resource Center
- Travel required
- Continuing education as required by GRaCE Resource Center
- Other duties as required (NOT giving rides!)

Role Play

Each group will develop a role play illustrating an ethical dilemma where a boundary has been crossed, for the rest of the class to take note. Once the role play has concluded, the performing group will 'fix' the crossed boundary.

- The role play will take place in a medical setting.
- Everyone will need to have a speaking part.
- Each role play will need to have a Recovery Coach Professional and coachee.
- Each role play will use the word "vacation."

You will have 20minutes to prepare.

Ethical Consideration in the Judicial System

The County Drug Court has a partnership with the GRaCE Resource Center to provide volunteer Recovery Coach Professional services. Bella the coach has been working with Christine (the coachee) for 10 months. During this time, Christine has shown progress and commitment to the program-starting a full-time job and planning on starting college in the fall part-time. Just before Christine's weekly urine test, Bella discovers Christine has smoked marijuana once during the past week. The County Drug Court policy is that relapse mandates a return to a 28-day inpatient treatment program, essentially starting the process over from the beginning. Bella does not believe this policy is in the best interest of her coachee for a variety of reasons.

Who is Bella ethically accountable to?

Who is Christine ethically accountable to?

Would it make a difference as to who Bella learned about the relapse from?

Thinking ethically, what action should Bella take? Christine take?

Recovery Coach Professional Judicial System Role Play

Your facilitator will assign one of the following role plays to your group.

Please use the words "more cowbell"

More Cowbell -SNL –YouTube

(1) The RCP is to appear at court and represent their coachee who has been invested and progressing in their drug court program. The RCP will act in an ethical, professional manner.

(2) The RCP is to appear at court and represent their coachee who has been invested and progressing in their drug court program. The RCP will *NOT* act in an ethical, professional manner.

(3) The RCP is to appear at court and represent their coachee who has *NOT* been invested and progressing in their drug court program. The RCP will act in an ethical, professional manner.

Recovery Coach Professionals are a model for healthy living.

Recovery Coach Professionals have a responsibility in creating, implementing, and sustaining methods that support their wellness in the following dimensions:

Emotional: the ability to cope effectively with life and build sustaining relationships with others.
Spiritual: related to values and beliefs that help one find meaning and purpose in life.
Intellectual: recognize one's unique talents and seek out ways to use knowledge and skills.
Physical: physical activity, healthy nutrition, and adequate sleep.
Environmental: the surroundings one occupies.
Financial: feeling of satisfaction about one's financial situation.
Occupational: satisfaction with one's choice of work.
Social: a sense of connectedness and belonging
Effective management of one's professional workload: including advocating for self-care when workload becomes a barrier.
Self-care: a top priority of the Recovery Coach Professional and the organization or businesses they provide services for.

Ending Exercise

Next Steps (Self-Care SMART Goal)

Come up with a "healthy-living" SMART goal that you will share in the chat box once you are back in the main room. You will have 10 minutes each to coach each other.

PROJECT FOR GRaCE SCHOLARSHIP CLASS PARTICIPANTS IN ADDITION TO THE REQUIRED 55 VOLUNTEER HOURS

Create a project increasing awareness of Recovery/Life Coaching and GRaCE that will have a lasting effect in YOUR community or context.

Email your completed plan within 10 days to GRaCEFacilitators@gmail.com for approval.

The project needs to be completed within 60 days.

Copyright © 2020, 2021, 2022, 2023 by Marti Steiner and John Unger
All Rights Reserved.

No part of this book may be used or reproduced by any means, graphic, electronic, or mechanical, including photocopying, recording, taping, or by any information storage retrieval system without the written permission of the publisher except in the case of brief quotations embodied in critical articles and reviews.

Third Edition

Made in the USA
Middletown, DE
26 May 2023

31069627R00064